FINALLY REVEALED:
The Inspiring Story of Rock Bottom to Business Success Any Entrepreneur (or Aspiring Business Owner) Can Follow to Improve their Business, Income, or Life...

From Prison to Prosperity

7 Lessons from an Ex-Con who Broke Free from Insurmountable Odds" to Create Success in Business, Family & Life *(And How You Can Do the Same)*

Mike Pisciotta

From Prison to Prosperity
7 Lessons From an Ex-Con who Broke Free from Insurmountable Odds"
to Create Success in Business, Family & Life *(And How You Can Do the Same)*

ISBN-13: 978-0692792919
ISBN-10: 0692792910

Published by
Pisciotta International, LLC
Melbourne, FL

Printed in the United States of America.

Table of Contents

Table of Contents

Introduction: Breaking Out of Your "Prison" and Chasing Success

If you're facing difficulty motivating yourself and accomplishing your goal of becoming successful as an entrepreneur, it's probably because you are being **restrained** by the shackles of the status quo.

Maybe you're stuck in a job you hate, taking orders from your boss. Maybe you have toxic family members, friends, or romantic partners who are holding you back.

They have you *tied down like a dog* and that's <u>EXACTLY where they want you to be.</u>

And your experience is absolutely no different than prison.

You may be stuck under financial obligations—facing 10 years of loan payments eating up everything you're earning now.

You may be a single parent with far more obligations, demands and bills than time in the day to climb out from under them all.

You might be trapped in a thankless job, another number to a big-wig CEO who doesn't know your name or appreciate what you bring to the table.

Every once in a while you're reminded of what success *could feel like*—new opportunities arise, you see them, maybe think about taking advantage of one—but you're always derailed by the *restrictions* holding you back...

The *chains you were born with.*

From the money in your bank account, to the opportunities you find—in many ways, you were born right into the situation you are in right now, am I right?

In many cases (and for many people) it's true. Very few people in this world move from one social class to another.

If you're born poor, you're likely to stay poor. If you're born rich, you're likely to inherit the money that keeps you rich.

That's the way our world works—**or does it?**

Let me share a story about my experience in PHYSICAL PRISON, so you can apply it to your life and break out of the status quo you've decided to leave behind. And yes, you should keep reading because in the 7 lessons I'm about to share, you'll see exactly how it is possible to create your ideal future **regardless** of where you are now.

Here's the story...

At age 18 I found myself in a jail cell with no idea of how I had gotten there, facing a very large prison sentence. After going back and forth for almost 2 years with the court system I was finally forced to accept a 10-year plea deal in lieu of the possibility of spending a lot more time behind bars.

My name is Mike Pisciotta and this is my story, "From Prison to Prosperity"...

I remember this one very pivotal day way back when I was just 19 with that long prison sentence ahead of me (8 ½ more years).

I was up inside my cell doing push-ups, exercising and reflecting on the road ahead and I vividly remember the internal conversation and commitment I made to myself, and God, inwardly saying, ***"They took 10 years of freedom, but I won't give them 10 years of LIFE."***

That small moment in time in an Orlando, Florida prison would completely transform and shape the trajectory of my life from that day forward.

As I moved through the prison system everyone around me was consumed with gambling, drugs, gangs and plain old negativity but I chose to immerse myself in God's Word, entrepreneurship, marketing and foreign languages (I learned to read, write and speak fluently; Spanish, Italian, French and Greek). Notice I said 'CHOSE'. This entire book is about the power that you possess and how your choices directly impact your life.

I was surrounded by haters, nay-sayers and negative people on every side, the *inmates wanted me to fail*, and <u>*guards wanted me to fail even more*</u>. This just fueled me to press harder, work harder and focus more.

During this time, I was counted as nothing more than a number.

I wasn't known as "Mike", but rather I was known by the number the state of Florida assigned to me at sentencing, "R18756".

Although I carried that label around with me, and had it beaten into my head every single day and on every possible occasion that I was merely a number, **I NEVER once accepted it**.

No matter how hard they tried to beat it into me or convince me that I was just another loser, **I NEVER once owned it**.

Sometimes it was challenging, since this label had to be worn on my chest at all times. I carried it with me everywhere. Seeing this badge every day and repeating my number at every count* helped create in me an unrelenting desire to never look back and never GO back.

Not only did I excel and overcome the odds but I smashed a status quo that had dictated failure to so many who had come before me. I broke a cycle of defeat for generations to come.

Don't ever let them tell you that you can't.

Don't ever let them tie you down.

Never be confined by the status quo.

You see, prison is much more than just a place or a punishment. ***It's a factory***.

In that factory, something is being produced and manufactured.

One side of the factory is kicking out worse criminals with deeper bitterness and hatred, while the other side is (rarely) kicking out **better, more focused and resilient people.**

The funny thing is, *we always had the choice as to which side we would emerge from.* The sad thing is, <u>most take the complacent route, never noticing what they are becoming until one day they just "are."</u>

It wasn't enough to ***want*** to be better, it required a consistent focus and diligence while every influence around you pressed harder and harder to bring out the worst.

Today, I'm no longer "R18756."

I'm better known as Mike, or Dad, as my two little ones (John & Sophia) would call me.

My story began when I was 18 years old and was given a 10-year prison sentence. During my time in prison, I developed the mindset, perspectives, and experiences that would shape me into the person I am today.

I learned several different languages, improved my physique, and studied business.

I even met my wife while in prison. *(That is an awe-inspiring story in and of itself that perhaps I'll share glimpses of later on in the book.)*

Following my release, I found that the philosophies I had developed were still just as relevant and continue to be to this very day.

My wife and I now run our own online marketing business and have done so for the past six years.

We went from having literally $40 in our bank account and selling trash on Craigslist to making 7-figures with a business model that practically runs itself, using the same exact mindset principles you're about to learn, and following the very same techniques, tips, and advice we teach our clients.

To date we have quite a few businesses, in several niches, some of which pull in around $70-$80,000 per month.

We have been blessed to be able to teach 4,431 paying students of our online training programs.

We have a Facebook Group filled with over 5,000 of the smartest, and most fun marketing-loving entrepreneurs hailing from 13 different countries.

We daily influence and reach over 30,000 people across social media.

The most humbling part is that we are overflowing with success stories of having helped thousands of people realize their own dreams of becoming internet marketing money making machines.

If you want to count yourself among these people, doing so is simple.

Just go to www.FromPrisonToProsperity.com/bonus and sign up for our free membership and Facebook group where you'll find loads of free resources to build your business.

My story is filled to the brim with hardships that still blow my mind looking back on them.

The moral is this:

You can overcome any hardship, achieve any dream, and conquer any obstacle. All you need to do is embrace the 7 lessons that I'm about to share with you.

Lesson 1: *Identify the Control You Have Over Your Life, Embrace It, and Prosper.*

September 10, 1999 started like any other day in my life. Little did I know at the time that it would actually 'the' day that would completely change the course of my life forever.

I woke up around noon like normal, dazed, still high from partying and drugging the night before. I got dressed and headed out in pursuit of the only thing that really mattered to me at the time, getting high. After meeting up with some friends and heading to a party for the night, we decided to get some Xanax bars and a few six packs of beer (not the best combination).

If you're not familiar with what Xanax is, in medical terms, it's a benzodiazepine. It's legally used for stress, anxiety and panic. However, 'on the street' it is used to get a feeling similar to intoxication. What sets Xanax apart from all the other miscellaneous drugs in the medicine cabinet, though, is its ability to make the user black out, the high chance of addiction and the fact that withdrawal from Xanax is potentially deadly.

Licensed clinical social worker Kirk Broaddus says, "Xanax is so dangerous because it hits you so fast, taking more and more in a short period of time can be lethal."

Mixing drugs with alcohol is dangerous in any case, but it is known to be especially dangerous with Xanax. Due to the fact that the two substances have the same effect on the body, they end up magnifying the feeling of intoxication to hazardous levels.

"If you mix alcohol with Xanax you're really playing with fire," Broaddus said.

What was meant to be a fun night of hanging out, turned into a perfect storm for disaster. Getting high and partying eventually fueled an all-night crime spree culminating in me (and two other 'friends') being dragged out of the back seat of a Chevy Impala, beaten up by police and waking up hand cuffed to a chair with a bright light shining in my face. Picture those old movies where the cop shines the hot light in the criminals face while he interrogates. Yeah, that bad!

I had no idea just how much this moment in time would shape the entire rest of my life.

September 11, 1999, *the following morning,* was the first day in my short 18 years on this planet that I had EVER taken personal responsibility for my life and the consequences of my choices.

That morning, *I woke up in a jail cell with absolutely NO recollection of the night before or why I was there.*

On the desk inside the cell was an official affidavit citing that I was being charged with 2 counts of armed robbery.

During the intoxicated spree the night before, myself and two other friends gallivanted around town at 2:00 am robbing store after store, and then eventually got caught by police at 5:00 am. I would later come to learn that I had taken 11 Xanax bars and consumed two six packs of beer and completely blacked out the entire night. When I awoke in the cell the officers advised me that I was extremely lucky to be alive and that they actually thought I had overdosed and wouldn't wake up.

As I paced around the cell and conversed with God, everything hit me like a ton of bricks.

I began to see clearly WHO I REALLY WAS and what my choices had led me to.

The truth is, as much as I hate to admit it, this night was *not* just one, isolated, misfortunate drug-induced mistake. It was more like the climax to a lifetime of bad behavior, mixed with a bad world view and mindset.

7

I was *really* a bad kid. I was medically diagnosed with ADHD (my case was even in some medical journal studies for it). I was out of control and next to impossible to discipline. Constantly in trouble, arrested multiple times, addicted to drugs, and involved in gangs.

Then you take my *already* terrible behavior and mix it with this: **It was never my fault.**

At least that was what I had been taught. The mindset exhibited in response to my bad behavior was that the ultimate responsibility always belonged to someone else. It was never me nor my choices that were to blame for the troubles I always found myself in. It was the teacher, the neighborhood, the cops, the principal, the judge, the _____ (insert any other reason you can think of) to blame for the poor decisions I had made and the circumstances I found myself in.

This is what I came to know. This was the world I grew up in. I had never heard or seen the principle of personal responsibility modeled, ever!

Most people face this problem—especially people struggling to find prosperity in their lives. For most folks who struggle through life, it's very often because they have never owned it.

What most people don't realize until it's too late (and what took a trip to prison for me to realize) is that **you are in complete control of your decisions.**

Not only that—you are responsible for the situation you're in today.

Life isn't something that just 'happens' to you. If that's what you have believed then it's time to shift that thinking and make some real changes.

One of the phrases I remember hearing from my Dad a lot as a kid was, "It's not what you know, it's *who you know*" (as said in his raspy Italian New Yorker voice).

I realize now that Dad was just repeating what he had heard and came to believe his whole life. It's really all he ever knew.

He would usually say this in response to, or regarding someone getting promoted, having success or advancing in life.

The perspective was that folks who have success achieve it by means other than hustle, knowledge and taking the right risks. It must've been luck, good family, or some kind of rubbing elbows with another rich person.

Dad was a respectable blue collar guy (a plumber) who worked hard my whole life, putting in 16 hour days when it was necessary. He was dedicated to the grind. The best work ethic you'd ever seen. His belief and experience had taught him that this was just 'how life was' and that riches were reserved for the lucky few, a system created beyond our control, not even attainable for the hard working regular folk.

As a kid, this was one of those things I always remember quietly questioning because it didn't seem to make sense.

I always had great respect for my Dad because of his commitment and hard work, but I also knew that something was *off* with the bigger picture of his world view.

I saw *tons of folks* succeed and rise based on what they knew. I saw examples of people with everything stacked against them still 'make it big'. It didn't add up to me.

That saying, "It's not what you know, it's who you know", would continuously echo in my mind almost every day of my 10-year prison sentence as the internal drive in me told me that I COULD succeed based on what I knew and that success wasn't just something for the lucky few.

You see, my Dad had accepted an idea that allowed him to settle and one which <u>welcomed an excuse</u>. An excuse which shifted personal responsibility away from himself onto external situations which he believed were outside of his control.

The truth is—nothing is "out of control."

Have you watched people just accept their "fate?"

Maybe they're staying in a dead end job they hate or taking orders from a slave driver boss all because they believe that is all there is.

I'm here to tell you that there IS more. You just have to go after it.

Have you seen people settle back, shift responsibility, and decide factors beyond themselves are in control of the situations they find themselves in?

You can't accept "fate."

If you do, you'll end up where I was before prison—you'll believe other people are responsible for your successes and failures.

Borrow this approach and put yourself in control...

You may not be in a *physical prison* like I was, but I want you to add up all the elements in your life that make you feel "trapped".

What's holding you back?

What elements are standing between you and success?

Where are you now and where do you want to be?

These are the exact questions that went through my mind while I sat in my prison cell.

I had come to believe with all my heart that where I was in life was a direct result of the choices I made and if I wanted to change my lot in life then I had to change my choices. Period.

Sounds pretty simple but it works.

It wasn't luck. It wasn't because of who I did or did not know.

It was because of _ME_.

This phrase played out in my mind over and over and it fueled me to press harder, learn more, apply myself deeper and break a cycle that wanted to crush me.

One of the first moments I can remember about waking up in that jail cell was the deep realization that I was there because of my own choices.

This was the very first time that I had to face this. ***The very first time that I was confronted with the truth of personal responsibility.***

When I finally 'woke up' in that jail cell, everything changed.

Perhaps what my Dad always said was right after all. Because once I came to know **myself** for who ***I really was*** everything changed and life became brand new.

The very moment I faced who I was, why I was there, and where I was, was the moment that everything changed.

Did the struggles disappear?

NO!

Did the challenges automatically dissipate?

Absolutely NOT!

What did change was ***how I approached those challenges and struggles***.

Initially it seemed like I was doomed to a life of crime and failure. It felt like this was all life had for me and that I would just become another 'number' in the system.

After 16 months of pleading, court appearances and postponed hearings, they went on to sentence me, just 19-years-old, to 10 years in Florida State Prison. This was what's called a 'mandatory sentence'. There was no good time*, no sentence shortening, no early release, nothing. Ten straight years. 3,650 days. In full.

This was more than half of my life at that time. Admittedly it seemed insurmountable. The odds were stacked against me. While all of my peers were heading off to college, getting married, and starting careers to begin life as an adult, I was heading to 'The Chain Gang to begin a 10-year mandatory sentence.

Although it felt extremely overwhelming and challenging I knew that I could overcome this and turn things around.

The guards and inmates all laughed and mocked my commitment to change and aspirations of greatness but it only fueled me even more (but hey, who's laughing now ?).

There is something incredibly powerful about taking personal responsibility.

Owning your choices and recognizing that where you are in life is a direct result of those choices.

It took me going to prison to recognize the most important lesson you'll take away from this book...

You are an individual and you have the individual power to break free from negativity, your self-constructed prisons, or circumstances you've come to believe aren't 'your' fault.

Now, whoever you are, whatever you want to accomplish, it's a fact that you have at least a few negative influences in your life.

Sadly, this weighs down a lot of people and *prevents them from taking the reins of their own life.*

When I went to prison in 1999, as an 18-year-old drug addict, I had come from a world, a home, and a lifestyle where these things were normal.

For the first 18 years of my life, all I was exposed to was a victim mentality, crime and drugs.

Drugs were common. **Failure was accepted** and life was something that happened **to** you.

There was no purpose or intention at all.

I didn't know anything outside of that small world I had been exposed to. It was all I'd ever seen.

I even started getting high with my own parents at just 14-years-old.

Now before we go any further, let me just make it very clear that my intention in sharing this is not to bash my family at all. I recognize that they did the best they knew how at the time. But it is important to show the full picture. It's important to see that my behaviors, my beliefs, my mindset, my surroundings, and my entire world view were deeply embedded in me, just as they were embedded in my parents, just as they are embedded in many others.

So this story is not meant to bash, it's meant to enlighten, inspire and empower. In order for that to happen, the real, raw, gritty truth of **patterns and strongholds** must be told.

Life is always about choices, no matter where you've come from.

And **it is possible** to create the life you want, no matter where you've come from.

So back to the story...

I dropped out of high school at 15-years-old. Ironically though, all of the years I did spend in the education system were spent in gifted classes. I always excelled at academics and was usually one of the smartest kids in the class. Unfortunately, **I had no direction or positive influence** to show me that there was a different path.

The prevalent mentality in my home was that success was unachievable and that the wealthy just had luck the rest of us didn't.

Even when I started changing my life and seeing glimpses of success my Dad would say things like, "You're one lucky son of a b**** Michael!" and make jokes about having me buy lottery tickets for him because of the 'luck' I had fallen into.

There was no connection to outlook creating overcomers, doctrine creating decisions, intentional action creating success. Life just is what it is. Some are the lucky privileged <u>few</u>.

Another lingering mentality in my life was the wealthy had to have attained their riches by unethical, illegal and evil methods. There was just no way to become *that* wealthy or successful without doing something terribly wrong or inheriting it. *It just wasn't normal.* It wasn't attainable. That's just the way it was.

It *wasn't* that people were paid according to the massive value they provided to the world. It was an anomaly. We **weren't** to respect it, desire it, or God forbid, work towards it... we were to resent it, fall in line, and accept our fate.

People in positions of leadership and authority were only out to promote themselves and keep the rest of us down. We were oppressed by the greedy.

There were a select group of people who drove the ship. You were not in control. Life just happened ***to*** you.

There was even an unspoken dark cloud that *something is wrong with you* or you were a *sellout* if you had the balls to believe **you** could be counted among these lucky, privileged (or evil) few.

Seeking to better yourself meant you thought you were better than others. Seeking to better yourself was a futile endeavor for a crazy person.

These influences and beliefs led me to a resentful, selfish, rebellious, and out-of-control lifestyle and a 10-year mandatory prison sentence by the time I was 18.

Similar influences and beliefs may not lead you to *physical prison* but a psychological one instead.

Here's an example...

Have you ever had someone you know and trust tell you "you can't do that?"

Perhaps a parent, a colleague, a friend—someone looking at your ambitions and lofty dreams saying "that's not the way the world works?"

This happens all the time to my clients...

You have a goal, an ambition, and a dream you want to pursue that just isn't satisfied by the same old 9 to 5 you were *born into,* but because of your upbringing, you've been told that wage-work job is the only way to make money, the only way to support yourself and your family...

When you tell your friends your dreams they look at your like you are crazy...

When you explain you want to start a business, make "passive income" or build something you can use to *break out and move up*, you just get blank stares.

This is all too common.

And it becomes a limiting factor on your success if you listen to it.

Thinking back to my prison experience...

After I woke up in that cell and began to reflect on who I was and where I had found myself, things started to dramatically change in my heart and my mindset.

Prison became a refuge for me. Prison pulled me out of a place, a world and a mindset that ***would have killed me.***

Prison allowed me the space to see things from a different perspective and be exposed to possibilities that I never knew existed.

I changed and became an individual, in control of my thoughts, actions, and future.

During these years of dramatic change and growth, one thing in my life didn't change.

My family. And most especially my mom.

They met my new found sense of self-improvement with an unexpected *resistance*.

I mean, you'd think my family would welcome the change with open arms. But it was quite the opposite and I found myself sad, angry and deeply confused as to why.

Although I tried to have influence and share the new life direction I had found, the faith in Jesus Christ that had changed me, it only fell on deaf ears.

The more I grew and changed, the more I tried to share with my family and I was continuously met with vicious comments. My mom (much more on her and how she has attacked us and tried to destroy our life later) would say things like this:

"YOU were the criminal. Not US!"

"You're the one who needs to change. We're fine the way we are."

This created a tremendous disconnect because I was growing as a person while my family was remaining stagnant behind an unwillingness to accept responsibility and make changes.

They felt it as well.

This obvious divide created much strife and resentment toward me as I continued to press on and reach for success.

My mother deeply resented who I had become and harbored a tremendous jealousy and resentment toward my now-wife Robin as if somehow she was the cause of this divide.

It was easier to shirk off what I shared because, hey I was just a low-life inmate, right?

When I walked out of prison, things didn't really change much. After all those years of trying to share and encourage, I began to see that there was a deep rooted issue present in my family that snowballed into resentment as I left prison and started to achieve some level of success.

You see, the man my parents had raised had become a criminal, a drug addict, a failure by most definitions but the man that emerged from that was just opposite and **she couldn't take any credit for it.** I can imagine that it was very challenging to face that truth.

Who I had become would only prove to be a *mirror reflecting back to her all that she was* (and was not).

Who I became over 10 years in prison was the very opposite of who I was raised to be and the reality of that truth must have been very hard to bear.

I had hoped that my life would bear witness to the possibilities available and that they would take responsibility for where they were in life and make changes, but she just attacked Robin and I.

I was always torn because I just couldn't understand why it was so hard for them to accept responsibility, repent and change. Especially when they could see it modeled it in my life. It wasn't just some 'inmate' preaching life-changing nonsense but they could now see it being lived out and creating success.

It blew my mind.

It was almost as if they *wanted* to struggle, be miserable and blame the world.

I never expected that my biggest haters at the time would be **my own mom**.

And while there may have been some differences in how my dad and I thought he never attacked us or came against us. My mom has vehemently attacked us, tried to destroy us has been the biggest adversary to our success.

It seemed as though each and every encounter with my parents, whether big or small, was an example of my inner mindset changes showing themselves in reality.

Whether a casual Thanksgiving get together, or a deep conversation, it always ended in conflict. Every glimpse of my resolve, awareness of personal responsibility, or choices being within our control made our division more obvious.

When any person sees this divide, they are really seeing **examples** that challenge and contradict their deep rooted beliefs. They are seeing **evidence** that the outlook which enabled them to create excuses may not be serving them. It cuts to the core.

When this divide becomes obvious, people tend to do one of two things. They're either thankful for the light and embrace a new world of possibilities... or they hate, attack, and try to remove the light because it exposes the darkness they are in.

Unfortunately, at this part of the story, she (my mom) chose the latter. Hatred, guilt and jealousy wreaked havoc. If something good happened in my life, it meant I was looking down on her. If I admired successful people, it meant I was embarrassed by her. Imaginary insults and offenses were constantly being revealed.

When I made choices not to allow their drug habits in my home or near my family, she would attack by reciting a long list of things they thought were 'wrong' with my life.

She was convinced that my 'bettered' self was a bad person. I was told that "I think I'm better than them" and "We didn't raise you this way". Every minor communication turned into conflict. Each conflict snowballed to the next.

Eventually my Mom went into a fury of attack toward both Robin and I. She viciously attacked us and ***even tried to use Facebook to destroy our up and coming business by private messaging all of our clients and colleagues and telling them that I was just a criminal and attempting to ruin us.***

She even went as far as to tell me that "prison ruined you and I should have had an abortion."

This was a very challenging time for us, but it also allowed us to develop real character, something we wouldn't trade for the world. It tested our resolve and commitment to the mindset we knew to be true.

Did it hurt?

You bet.

Did it break us?

Nope.

It only made us **_stronger_**.

After things finally settled a few years later things turned around with my parents.

My parents also went on to face their own struggles in life when my Dad was diagnosed with stage 4 throat cancer in June of 2014. Their entire world was shaken. Dad had been the bread winner my entire life and now he was facing a fight that would disable his ability to provide and challenge him like nothing else he had ever seen.

Both Mom and Dad fought the cancer as Dad endured the rigors of chemo therapy over 6 months. Every week was a fight and it seemed the news from the doctors changed with each treatment. One week it was looking good, the next not so good. Dad fought the cancer and thankfully overcame the disease.

Dad is now in full remission taking it one day at a time. The cancer seemed to be a rock bottom place for him that changed how he looked at life. Sometimes it takes rock bottom, waking up in jail, being diagnosed with a terminal illness, being fired from a job after 20 years or whatever it is you may be facing, to wake us up and call us out of the 'cloud' we live in.

I write this book with the hopes that you can see your possibilities in the now, *without* the need for things to get worse, or face your version of rock bottom.

As I've often looked back at the journey of 10 years in prison, a dysfunctional upbringing, extreme opposition, shut doors, obstacles, vicious attacks from my own mom, I've found that these are *the things that have fueled me.*

You can use the same negativity as fuel.

Whenever someone says you that you can't, you need to recognize your power as an individual to make it happen.

You may be all alone without a glimpse of support (or even with vicious haters)...

You may have been raised to *expect and accept* a certain level of status, of wealth, or life...

You may even have very real obstacles or crippling limitations looming over you...

But that doesn't mean you are stuck there.

You have the power to break out of your own prison, embrace your potential to change, and move forward on the path you choose.

And you can't let any person, thought, or circumstance stand in your way!

Lesson 2: Prison is Just a State of Mind: *You Can Break Out of Anything with the Right Mindset*

Taking control of the choices you make is an essential part of escaping the prison *you've constructed for yourself* and achieving personal and financial prosperity.

But I'm often asked, "How do you *actually take control?*" After all, just saying "I'm going to make better choices" and actually doing it are two fundamentally different things.

Here's what I always say:

If you want to better yourself, you need to accept that your current way of thinking about the world is *fundamentally flawed.*

Prison is a mindset!

Yes, what I discovered is that *even physical prison* is a mindset! And your own personal prison—the one *you've created* and trapped yourself in with *manmade, philosophical, and thought-based* obstacles telling you "I can't do this" and "I don't have the knowledge to do that..."

Your *personal prison* is also a mindset you create for yourself.

For the first 18 years of my life, the mindset and way of thinking I was taught and exposed to led to my incarceration in a physical prison.

I realized though, ***that I had really been in prison <u>all those years</u> long before it had manifested physically***.

During my 10-year sentence, I was keenly aware that if I ever wanted to change the direction of my life it would have to start in **the way that I was thinking**.

While most guys focused on either a few outward behaviors or even worse, becoming better criminals, my focus was always on recreating the way I thought about, processed and reacted to life.

It's hard to believe, but I witnessed literally hundreds, if not thousands, of guys leave prison only to return a few months later with more time, new stories <u>and more excuses</u>. It baffled me.

I also remember speaking to several old timers* who had gone back and forth, in and out of the system, some as many as **11 times!**

These guys were serving a life sentence on the installment plan (2 years here, 4 years there, 8 years here) and they couldn't see why.

My confusion led me into some very interesting conversations with many of these guys and I could ALWAYS spot a common thread immediately.

Prison was in their ***MINDS*** and they just couldn't see it.

I would often try to share this truth but it fell by the wayside, even while they all noticed something different about me and how I lived my life amongst them. Many just couldn't receive this simple truth.

When I was released from prison, I found this same dilemma in many of my family members. They too, had been in prison, many for a lot longer than I had. What baffled me was the inability to see it and change it.

A person must WANT to break free.

They MUST want to be released from prison!

They have to want it more than anything or they will settle for the prison life while convincing themselves, "Hey, this isn't that bad after all."

Maybe you can relate. Maybe things really aren't that bad after all. Perhaps the minor comforts have allowed you to settle for less than the best.

Here's the key to changing your mindset and breaking free:

Realize no matter where you are now, you can *escape* by shifting how you think and transforming your mindset.

Until the very day you leave this earth, you have an opportunity to start over each and every day.

You can make the choice to start over and escape no matter where you are right now.

It might be difficult to see. It might be hard to believe that you can claw your way past the obstacles you are facing—the *prison* surrounding you.

Your prison may be business struggles—not knowing the tools you need to start your business, the inability to come up with new ideas, difficulty mapping a plan for the future.

You might find people who pull you down, a world telling you "no you can't" filled with non-believers in your vision of the future.

Your prison may be guilt for consecutive bad choices you have made.

Or maybe personal struggles like financial instability or depression keep you trapped.

Perhaps it's a combination of all of these factors.

Whether you're in the middle of the darkest period of your life like I was, or you're just facing some small potholes in your road ahead, ***nothing is set in stone***. Say it with me, "Nothing is set in stone."

Many times I overhear Robin telling our 5-year-old son John that he can start over every second. She tells him, "Snap your fingers! See how fast that is? You can make a better choice just like that!"

Robin tells me she can literally see it in his eyes when he has been in his personal prison that it starts to ***define*** him rather than *shape* him. Almost like he feels doomed to continue on this path or that it means he is just 'a bad kid' and 'that's just the way it is' without realizing that **he can choose better** at any moment.

You see, John has a strong connection to good choices, develops a powerful mindset and remembers his life lessons better because he experiences the cause and effect of choices. So his little 5-year-old prisons are part of what shapes him, the good and the bad are instrumental parts of who he becomes.

It's important to <u>recognize</u> your prison. The danger to avoid is letting your prison stick with you in a way that keeps you stuck. You want to let it stick with you in a way that shapes you and affects **lasting change**.

Just a few days before I was released from prison, I was impelled to write my future, free, self a letter.

As my sentence was nearing an end, one of the things I felt to be most important was to NEVER forget where I had come from. Prison was a part of me. It was a part of who I was and who I would become.

I felt very strongly that no matter what successes I would see in life ahead it was imperative that I never forgot where I had been and the other guys I had left behind who needed to see someone *break the cycle.*

In my letter (pictured below), I reminded myself of a certain story from the Bible about 10 lepers who had ALL been healed of leprosy by Jesus. But of the 10 who had been healed ONLY one came back to say thank you.

As I wrote to my future self, I reminded myself to NOT be like the other 9 but **to be the one who came back and said thank you**.

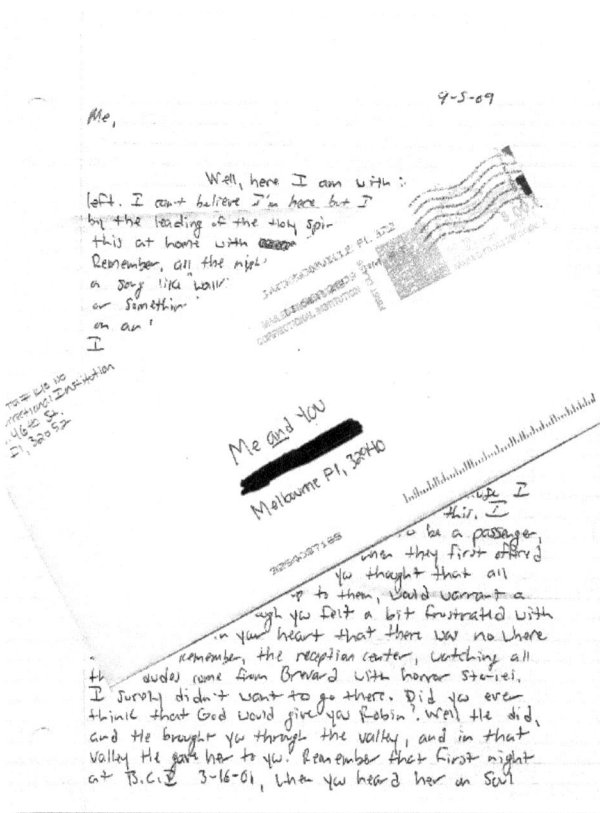

As a
resu
lt of that letter, I've had the great privilege of inspiring hundreds
of inmates to see that success is possible and that *__failures in life
are just another chance to start over__*.

Whether you've failed at life (like I did) or failed at business, at
home or wherever, *there is always another chance to start over.*

Let me share another story about my time at a particular prison
facility, Brevard Correctional Institution.

Brevard was notorious for extreme violence and gang activity.
Even the guards were scared to work there. They didn't call it
Gladiator School for nothing.

One day, this young Spanish guy came in with all his stuff to fill the empty bunk beneath me. I immediately recognized him because he was well known as being the leader of the Latin Kings.

His name was Vidal (nicknamed Coco) and he was a very troubled young man. We talked a lot about God, life, politics, you name it. He was extremely intelligent and it always amazed me that *he chose to apply his intelligence to moving drugs and masterminding gang activity.*

He often explained to me that the gang lifestyle was all he knew. He believed he didn't have any other choices. He was in a prison in his mind because it was all he knew.

I'll never forget the conversations we had and the perspective I gained on life as our conversations allowed me to dig deep into myself and analyze life from all angles. (I, myself, was only 19 at the time so I had a lot to learn.)

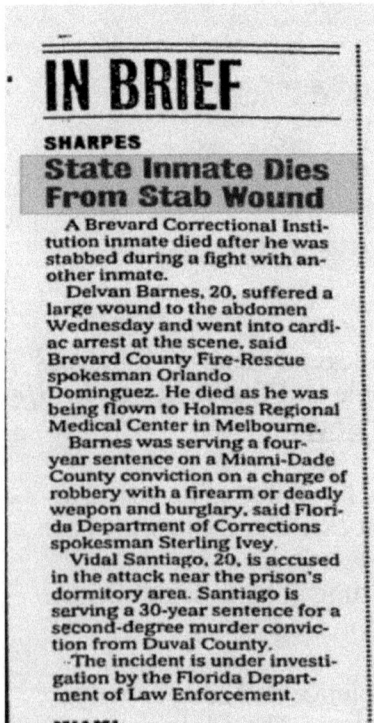

It also strengthened the resolve I had in me. The resolve that burned deep in me telling me that I always had a choice. **Always**. Despite what my environment dictated. I had the choice to let it (prison and the circumstances) break me or let it make me.

I left that institution in March of 2003.

Within a month of leaving, I heard through the prison grapevine (and later confirmed by Robin) that Coco had killed a 20-year-old inmate.

The news really hit home (see the newspaper clipping).

IN BRIEF

SHARPES

State Inmate Dies From Stab Wound

A Brevard Correctional Institution inmate died after he was stabbed during a fight with another inmate.

Delvan Barnes, 20, suffered a large wound to the abdomen Wednesday and went into cardiac arrest at the scene, said Brevard County Fire-Rescue spokesman Orlando Dominguez. He died as he was being flown to Holmes Regional Medical Center in Melbourne.

Barnes was serving a four-year sentence on a Miami-Dade County conviction on a charge of robbery with a firearm or deadly weapon and burglary, said Florida Department of Corrections spokesman Sterling Ivey.

Vidal Santiago, 20, is accused in the attack near the prison's dormitory area. Santiago is serving a 30-year sentence for a second-degree murder conviction from Duval County.

The incident is under investigation by the Florida Department of Law Enforcement.

Choices. Choices. Choices.

A few months later, I learned that Coco had taken his own life while awaiting trial in the county jail.

This hit home even harder.

During the months we spent together, we really bonded and I believed in my heart that he truly wanted a way out. He just couldn't find it.

As I reflected on the time we spent together, tears rolled down my cheeks and the fire in my heart to **break the cycle** and emerge victorious only grew stronger.

Several months ago I had the privilege of returning to Brevard C.I. (now shut down) to shoot some video for the release of this book... as I stood inside that prison, it felt surreal. I could feel what it was like all over again. I could hear the keys on the guards' belt clanging around as if it were yesterday, I could feel the oppression in the air. It brought me back.

It also helped me to remember that *I still had a choice.*

Every day, I have a choice. We all do. Question is...

What are you doing with yours?

Are you simply waiting around for something to happen? Sitting, content with were you are now?

Or are you taking actionable steps forward, making choices for yourself, and reframing your state of mind?

Lesson 3: How to Find Your Mindset, Overcome Adversity, and Stay Focused

Overcoming adversity is NOT EASY.

That's why it's always important to take a step back and reflect on your situation. When you think to yourself that you have a choice in *how* these roadblocks are going to affect you, they will be easier to put behind you.

Prison taught me many valuable life skills that have carried over to almost every area of my life now.

The prison environment is **designed to keep you down**. When one inmate tries to excel and break from the norm, it makes them a target. It welcomes all of the others (who still desire to live the same way and pursue negativity) to attack, mock and ridicule you.

The world outside of prison is pretty similar (except the food is just a little better). As you embark on your personal path to success, you're going to encounter 'haters', situations, and obstacles *determined to keep you down.*

You'll be starting up a mountain between where you are now and where you want to be, realizing the enormity of what you're about to undertake—and throughout it all, you'll have people trying to bring you down.

They may be peers who say you can't do it, competitors who try to stop you, even a family that doesn't support your dreams.

Each time you do face adversity, **I want you to think about the two choices most people make:**

They either try to *get better* at the only thing they know.

OR

They numb themselves to reality and just "get by".

What you have to do is **choose to be different.** Don't settle for one of the two most common ways people deal with adversity and obstacles in their lives, careers, and work.

Thinking back to my experience in prison, this is exactly the mindset that helped me make it out and make something of myself.

Staring up the mountain at a 10-year prison sentence (or staring up at a bold goal you've set for yourself).

It might be hard for the average person to imagine all the feelings, fears, questions and unknowns that come along with such a situation.

"Am I going to survive this?"

"Will it ever be over?"

Being only 18 years old made it that much more daunting.

I very keenly remember thinking and feeling that, "this is more than half of my life so far" and "what the heck am I going to do at 28 years old starting from scratch?"

At times, those thoughts and feelings tried to **overwhelm and discourage me**, as they would anyone.

However, there were several things I learned throughout that journey that I believe helped set me up for success upon release.

The prison environment is like its own self-contained world. A world where most of the guys who surrounded me were focused on 1 of 2 things:

Being better criminals.

OR

Numbing the daily life and trying to forget where they were.

Usually guys who had as much time to do as I did would completely disconnect from the outside world because it was too hard and painful to stay connected. It was just easier to accept prison as your new world.

I mean what good would staying connected really do for you?

What good would learning about the new iPhone, what a 'Tweet' is or 'how to share a photo on Instagram' really do for someone in prison?

It only reminded you of all that you were missing out on and how quickly the world outside was speeding past you.

And this was where **I CHOSE to be different!**

It was a choice. A tough choice because it made things a little more challenging. Instead of the easy road of 'numbing myself' I chose to stay in touch.

Instead of losing touch and trying to forget the outside world I PURPOSEFULLY sought to stay connected, up to date and in touch with the real world.

At times, it made life much more challenging because it amplified just how fast things were moving and how much of a disadvantage I would be at upon release. But, it also *drove me.*

10 years of intense focus on 1 GOAL, 1 specific goal of FREEDOM helped me to develop an **unrelenting resolve that became the catalyst for success when I left that world behind**.

While the other guys were gambling, getting high, joining gangs and wasting their time, I was working diligently to stack the deck in **my favor**.

I didn't realize it at the time, but that focused resolve carried over into life on the other side of those fences.

While I found that there are so many distractions out here and way more things pulling at someone in the free world than there are on the inside, that daily habit helped me to FOCUS! To FOCUS on the one goal at hand.

FREEDOM!

I firmly believe that focus is one of the most important skills an entrepreneur (or anyone for that matter) can develop and hone on a daily basis.

There are so many things to distract you (especially in this world of online business) but you have to know your purpose and FOCUS!

You have no excuses at all. If this dude (me ☺) could walk out of a Florida prison after 10 years to face a world that mercilessly sought to pass him by and still create massive success...

WHY CAN'T YOU???

Picture a bucket full of crabs and *one of those guys trying to get out*. **All the others are trying to pull him back in**. That is exactly what it is like on the inside.

I spent almost every waking moment on *self-improvement*, whether it was business study, Biblical study, finance, foreign language, or personal fitness. No matter what it was, this daily choice to live different, to change my life and change how I viewed the world attracted a <u>massive hoard of haters</u>.

<u>*I realized that I had a choice, a choice to let them break me or MAKE me.*</u>

I chose the latter.

At times it became more challenging than others especially when that choice went against the inner code or "what is expected" nonsense.

Every afternoon around 1:00 pm the weight coach would come into the institution and open up the weight pile for all of us to go in and use the weights to work out. Because there was a very limited supply of weights, each inmate would have to sign out 1 set each. This made it very important to be one of the first guys at the fence if you wanted to get anything worthwhile.

Well, this group of haters *actually paid other guys to beat me* to the fence and sign out all the weights just so I couldn't use them. I would have to wait hours sometimes.

And I always had a choice.

Let it break me or let it MAKE me. I could let the challenges and frustrations control me or let them shape me into what I needed to be successful.

I chose the latter.

And so can you!

We all have choices to make and challenges to face every day no one is exempt. Success comes when you let those challenges MAKE you instead of break you!

Be different, stand out no matter what, and decide not to simply settle for mediocrity or give up on your dreams!

If you decide to let your experiences make you instead of break you, you need to have outlets to divert your attention to.

You can't use what the haters do to you as fuel if you don't know where you're heading, am I right?

During my 10-year tenure in the 'Chain Gang', I sought to utilize every single opportunity presented to me.

I took **every class** and **read every marketing**, **business** and **personal development book** I could get my hands on.

I became a certified **Sous Chef**, I learned **marketing, sales, personal training, how to start a restaurant business, real estate, and even the stock market.**

One thing I knew for sure is that there would be no way for me to predict what I would do once I left prison, but I knew for certain that I had to prepare myself for any and every opportunity that would present itself.

Always having my nose in a book or doing some sort of studying attracted a lot of negativity from the guards who would often deride me and say things like:

"You're wasting your time INMATE. All that learnin' ain't gonna do you no good. You'll be back in less than a year"

They would even go so far as to <u>search my locker area</u> and <u>take my books away just to spite me</u> and make me have to go through a long process to get them back.

But I always had a choice and YOU always have a choice too.

Yes, there are plenty of obstacles in my story—people trying to *take away my opportunity to learn* and grow...

You'll face many of the very same obstacles on your journey to transforming your life.

But after you are able to use the obstacles you face as motivation, you will stop viewing them as CHALLENGES.

Your ambition will begin to take charge and you will view "challenges" as NECESSARY PREREQUISITES FOR SUCCESS!

Throughout the time I spent in prison, one of the jobs I had the longest was being a diet cook in the kitchen (yes, inmates have all kinds of dietary needs... Kosher, Halal, Vegan, etc...)

This was one of the few jobs where you worked for an outside company as opposed to guards. The company that handled the food service was called Aramark and they didn't have the best hiring practices.

We were forced to work for people who had never experienced an ounce of authority in their lives who were now given ultimate authority.

Anything they said would be law. I'm sure you can imagine just how well that went over.

I remember this one particular lady who really hated me (because she was in a relationship with one of the inmates who really hated on me big time) and she would <u>continuously go out of her way to disrespect me or make me do the worst jobs in the kitchen.</u>

There was an intense attitude of disrespect and lording over the inmates *just because they could.* This lady would 'try' (disrespect) the inmates daily in the most demeaning ways, almost like it was for fun, or to get some kind of sick pleasure out of it. I even witnessed this lady pouring tea all over an inmate in the spirit of 'you are beneath me and I will treat you as I please'.

One day I got real tired of the abuse and went to speak to the lieutenant (he was head of the institution at the time) about the situation and how she was treating most of us. Turned out that not only did she lie but she actually got her minion inmates (some of whom I was looking out for) to lie for her, leaving me as the only one telling the truth in a world where truth isn't valued.

I was given the option to recant my story or go to confinement.

At that moment, I realized that my values and integrity were at stake. I'd spent years working on this area of my life and now it was being tested.

This could be a challenge or an opportunity to learn and move forward.

I chose the latter and they put me in handcuffs and took me off to jail* (yes, confinement is "jail" within prison).

No sunlight. No communication with the outside world. No access to anything at all.

When I got to confinement I was pretty pissed off and embittered about the whole thing as you can imagine.

But I always had that choice.

From Prison to Prosperity

When I got to my cell, the cellmate I had was a 20-year-old kid (heck I was only 24 at the time) whose only aspirations in life were climbing the ranks of his gang. We didn't get along very well at first, but over the weeks he saw me maintain a consistent routine of *exercise, bible reading, and studying* that awakened him to a completely different perspective on life.

I'm not sure where that young man is today but I know for certain that <u>he left confinement with a different perspective</u>.

Sometimes the things we face aren't always for us or about us. Sometimes those things help to make us who we need to be for someone else.

Embrace the challenges and let them MAKE you!! (Someday someone may just thank you!)

Lesson 4: How to Set and Accomplish Your Goals

A lot of people don't achieve their goals.

And it's not because they don't *want to*, it's because they don't *try to*. And when I say 'try' I don't mean attempt and give up. I mean full on hardcore, no stopping effort.

It's essential for people to **take action** when a situation for growth presents itself. Otherwise, your dreams will pass you by and the haters will be proven right.

It's up to you!

If you start looking for opportunities today, **you'll find new goals everywhere around you.**

All you have to do is *take action* when the opportunities for personal and financial growth seek you out.

In 2004, I had the great privilege of meeting a young man named Tyrone, who inspired and challenged me.

We were at a prison work camp and Tyrone was one of those guys who spent his *every waking moment on self-improvement and personal development.*

I was drawn to him because I knew he had taught himself to read, write and speak Spanish (among other languages and skills) and I knew he had taught a few others as well. Unfortunately, he wasn't looking to teach anymore as he told me that no one would follow through and he would just wind up wasting time.

Day after day, I would try to convince him to teach me. After months of trying to persuade and convince him, I was finally able to convince him to teach a Spanish class and I devoured everything he taught me. So much so that within 9 months, *I was completely fluent in reading, writing and speaking and I even began offering my own classes.*

This was my first real "Entrepreneurial" moment.

During the class that he taught, I was the ONLY one who applied what I had learned and valued what he was teaching. The others just loved the idea of learning, but never really applied themselves to actually retain and master what they were learning. The 'idea' of learning was enough to make them 'feel' like they were actually accomplishing something when in fact they weren't accomplishing anything at all.

After I became fluent, I had a large number of guys wanting *me* to teach *them*.

The entrepreneur in me rose up and decided to create my own training program utilizing a specific method I had developed for learning languages. This system would guarantee that ANYONE would learn within 6 months.

Along with that, I knew that if I offered it for free no one would value the teaching. So, I charged a small weekly fee (in prison we pay for things with Ramen noodle soup and tuna packets).

It was my first lesson in entrepreneurship. Out of the 10 guys who paid to learn, half of them actually applied themselves, and of those, 50% of them learned the language and retained what they learned. Much greater results this time around then the class that I learned in.

This was just the beginning of my 'inmate enterprising'.

Several months later, I got a letter from Robin during mail call and the envelope had a cloud design on the outside as opposed to the standard white regular envelopes. Several other inmates asked me about the envelope wanting some of their own to send out to their families.

Opportunity slapped me in the face (again).

I knew if I was going to be successful as an entrepreneur someday then I needed to learn how to sell (sales skills are extremely important in almost every area of life) and these guys, on the inside, needed stationary. Perfect mix.

That night, when I called Robin, I explained the discovery I had made and had her send me a package with several types of envelopes and stationary. I figured out the cost, demand and what I would need to be profitable.

Within just a few days, I was up and running, selling like mad and stacking ramen noodle soups, tuna packets and cheese squeezes to the ceiling.

I now had an "inmate enterprise" that allowed me to hone and develop the number one skill I knew I needed... SALES.

Demand rose dramatically and I also had special order requests come in for colors, holiday patterns, etc... I was the inmate version of Hallmark.

That experience taught me a ton about entrepreneurship.

The most valuable lesson that I learned in this was ***how to spot a profitable opportunity***.

And when I say profitable, I am not only referring to the monetary side because at that time the "money" wasn't my greatest need. Sales skills were.

Sometimes the most profitable things for us and our businesses is the development of a skill or the lessons only experience can teach us.

Along with that, I also quickly realized that **obstacles** and **challenges** *are most often just opportunities in disguise.*

It doesn't matter where you are or what circumstances you are faced with.

You always have a choice to apply yourself, dig deep and seize opportunities. Closed doors, hundreds of "no's" and all the nay-sayers in the world can only do 1 of 2 things. It will either crush you and your dreams OR it will become the fuel that powers you forward to accomplish and realize your dreams. Choice is yours.

Setting your goals is easy once you open your eyes and take advantage of the opportunities around you.

If you decide to let your experiences *make you* and zero in on progressing your life forward, you are bound to come across some positive experiences amidst the overwhelming sea of negativity.

When you find these moments, it's important to cherish them and appreciate what they mean to your life.

Not only will it make your journey easier in the immediate future, *but it can also lead to better experiences down the road* (as was the case with me)!

One reason people don't succeed in achieving their goals is because they lack confidence to even start in the first place.

This is the easiest place to "go wrong."

Most people just don't trust themselves to make *good decisions*.

They don't believe that their lives *can actually get better*.

However, if you begin to realize that you are actually *headed somewhere GREAT* and that you have a positive impact on the people around you, you will start to develop a **much stronger sense of self-worth.**

The way to announce your self-worth to the status quo that you have rejected and to all the other hardships you have faced is to ***TRUST YOUR GUT!***

When Robin and I first started writing each other and communicating back and forth I was very, very adamant about NOT trying to get into some "prison relationship."

I knew that I had over 8 years left and it would just be extremely selfish on my part to try and go down that road.

After a few months of writing, it became glaringly obvious that there was a divine appointment in us meeting and the signs were clear.

Robin set it up to come and see me with a special visit.

Now, Robin was scared to death. Not just of prison, but of meeting me in person.

And I definitely did a great job at making her more nervous by joking and elaborating on the apparent awkwardness and such. The girl was a wreck, so she wanted to bring a friend along to kind of break the ice (but God had a different thing in store).

When she arrived at the prison, they called me to come up and when I get there, all the guards were laughing. They were telling me that she couldn't get in because the paper work didn't make it over from classification and only her friend, Marcel, could get in. Talk about frustration!

When they opened the door to the visitation area, I caught the first glimpse of Robin in person on the other side of the glass and it was at that moment that we both knew.

We knew this was for real and we knew that we were meant to be.

Our relationship began because I *trusted my gut* to let me know that this was going to be *for the best.*

The road was being paved even while we were completely unaware of where it would lead. We just followed.

Funny thing is, all of this was unfolding in the least likely of places and in the very place that I, myself, would have paid to avoid.

You, too, may be in one of those places facing similar choices.

If you are, know this...

Take advantage of the opportunities in front of you, let your goals arise organically (they will), and trust your gut instinct.

Lesson 5: Be Thankful for Your Past - *And Then Leave It Behind*

There is no such thing as a *bad experience* in life. We may feel like things are 'bad' but I firmly believe that where we are and more importantly 'who' we are is directly related to our experiences.

As mentiooned in the earlier chapters I've had to deal with the challenges that come along with having a psychotic mom. While many would look at that as a 'bad' experience or an obstacle I deeply recognize it as one of the key things have helped shape me into who I am today.

As a matter of fact, during the last rounds of edits for this book I was faced with another 'attack'. While on vacation with my family in Washington, DC, my parents came along to enjoy the trip with us. Robin and I had allowed my mom to come back into our lives, even against our better judgement, because she used my dad as a pawn to control and manipulate. If we didn't speak to or communicate with her than she would see to it that we had no contact with my father. The deep level of control and manipulation involved was unlike any other I had seen, even after 10 years in prison.

My wife and I were saddened and hurt by the fact that my dad was forced to miss out on seeing his grandchildren grow up and because of this we decided to allow her back. Unfortunately, it didn't take long for a situation to arise and for the 'inner monster' to rear its ugly head, sadly it just so happened to be while we were all on vacation in DC.

On day 3 of our trip, in Washington DC, she started a big fight with us for no reason and it quickly escalated. While Robin and I tried to keep our distance (even though we were sharing a house and a vehicle as part of our road trip) we thought she could be a civil adult and go on to enjoy the trip. Boy were we wrong. My father did all he could to try and keep her from us and to keep her from assaulting and harassing us but it didn't work. She literally followed us around the city and even in the National Museums heckling, harassing and attacking us despite the fact that we completely ignored her (which only made her more angry and irate).

As it continued to escalate she spit on us several times, called us every name under the sun and just made life miserable for everyone. It hurt me deeply because I could see the pain and hurt in my father's face as he knew where it was headed. I told him that I didn't want to have to leave her behind but I also had to be proactive in protecting my family and my sanity. While he understood and tried his best he couldn't keep her from attacking us and harassing us at every corner. No matter what we did she would follow right behind us harassing and creating a horrible situation for both us and our children.

On the way to the parking garage to get our truck to head from DC to NY she blew up in the Uber (poor Chinese guy was scared to death) and she told Robin she was calling DCF to have our children taken away. If you're a mom reading this then you can relate to what that felt like for Robin and it was then that the proverbial 'camel's back' was broken. I told my dad I was done and she was not, by any means, getting into my vehicle or coming any further with us. In his anger he yelled at her as he knew it was her fault that he was now in a position to find a way back home to Florida.

At the apartment where we all had to get our things and go our ways she attacked us again, spitting on us, attacking us, trying to create a physical altercation (which thank God didn't happen) and even began pouring water all over the furniture to try to destroy the apartment.

After my dad was able to get her out of there she began the assault by way of text and sent Robin and I things that would only make you cringe as a human... She has told us it is now her life's mission to ruin us and everything we know.

Hurtful? Sure.

Debilitating? Absolutely not!

Fuel? Yup, you bet!

I've learned that life is 2-fold, just like a coin. There's always two sides. Sometimes things are lovely, the sky is blue, unicorns deliver you sherbert *:p* and the sun shines on your face... And sometimes things are gray and it seems like everything is to your contrary. But you see life is life. And it's the things we face, both good AND bad that make us who we are... Only difference between the successful and the not successful is how they choose to react to life, because LIFE happens to all of us.

The good, the bad and the ugly ALL are contributing to WHO you are... Only question is, "Who are YOU letting it make you?"

Many people are bogged down by traumatic events that have occurred to them. Unfortunately, this often contributes to their *lack of success.*

When I walked out of prison at 28-years-old, I entered a world that had not waited for me.

Life had continued. People grew up. Technology advanced. And there were several times when I would be around other folks my age and feel like I was way behind, out of touch and just wouldn't ever catch up.

I mean, they had a 10 year jump start on me, right?

Well at least it appeared so on the outside. I can tell you, it could have been very easy to fall into that way of thinking. To foster the thoughts that I was too far behind, everyone my age was already established and blah, blah, blah... but then I started to realize that those thoughts and ideas weren't exclusive to me and my situation.

<u>*Almost everyone has someone else they compare themselves to.*</u>

The first few months were **by no means easy**. I had a lot to learn, but I also had this deep sense of *thankfulness. Thankful to be free.* I was even *thankful to be able to walk into a Wal-Mart* (go figure, right?) and that thankfulness drowned out the feelings and thoughts of being way behind.

Instead of focusing on where I wasn't, I began to focus on where I wanted to be.

Robin and I knew one thing very clearly; we **didn't want to waste time**.

We knew that we didn't really have time to make a whole lot of mistakes, so we focused.

Whatever endeavor we were a part of, we were all in. 100%. Fully committed. Completely devoted. And within a year or so we found ourselves far ahead of our peers.

We started out very scrappy at first just trying to pay the bills. We poured every dime we had into building an online business because we knew that it would provide the freedom we so craved. After turning and burning on that business we had grown it into the multiple 6-figure a year mark and were pretty comfortable.

It was in those moments that I started to become **thankful again. Thankful for prison**.

You see the very thing that was designed to destroy me, to cripple me, to hinder me, turned out to be the very thing that would catapult me into much more than I ever would have seen on my own.

No matter what life hands us, the challenges we face or the feelings of defeat or failure that try to cripple our movements we ALWAYS have a choice.

We all want the same thing in life. *We want to be* **happy.**

But, where does happiness come from? A sense of *fulfillment*.

Yet, most people don't feel like their living a fulfilling and happy life. Why is this?

Because they haven't learned to ***value their time!***

One of the things I remember most from growing up was my Dad's commitment to work.

I remember hearing and watching him often share with pride how he "would go into work sick, injured, tired, on holidays, no matter what." To him, it was badge of honor to "never miss a day."

He came from a very blue collar, hardworking background and this was the general measure of worth for a man... How hard he worked.

I was also keenly aware that his commitment to work often superseded his commitment to family.

If there was ever a choice between the two, work would always win out with the common explanation being, "I gotta do what I gotta do" and "we need the money".

As I grew up watching this, I also noted that this same level of commitment toward his job was **never** reciprocated by any of these jobs he held.

Being a plumber his entire life saw him bounce around from job to job at times, and although he carried this commitment with him, it was never matched by any of his employers.

No matter how committed my Dad was to his job or his boss they never seemed to extend this same level of loyalty and commitment. I'm sure it was extremely frustrating for him. I mean he gave these jobs his all and oftentimes he'd find himself without work for no apparent reason at all.

After so many years I wondered, "how long is this going to be the case?"

"How long is he going to continue to choose his job over <u>family</u>, <u>life</u> and <u>freedom</u>?"

Growing up I always wondered, "when <u>are</u> we going to be able to *afford* it?"

Even when things seemed to be going well financially I still always heard that phrase in response to most things in life. And it became clear to me that 'affording' something or not wasn't really the issue at all. Mindset was. It was almost as if the phrase, "We can't afford it" was the easy excuse whether it was really true or not.

It never made any sense to me and it created a very deep **internal commitment to value my time more than anything** when it came time for me to have a family.

I never wanted to be the guy who consistently chose work over family or anything in life that matters.

I think watching him make this choice over all those years kind of made me mad. Mad that he allowed himself to be duped into believing the lie that one day this level of commitment would be magically appreciated and he would somehow achieve *financial freedom*. Mad because I knew he was giving his all, working his butt off and pouring in to something that just didn't appreciate the effort in return. I'm not sure whether he ever really thought that or if he was just doing the only thing he knew to do.

Although he never intended it, watching him make this choice all those years, and be constantly busy taught me an immensely valuable lesson and helped create in me the *entrepreneurial fire that burns today*.

When I walked out of prison, I didn't know exactly what I wanted to do but I DID know what I DIDN'T want to do. I vowed to NEVER allow myself to be a **slave** to someone else for **a few bucks** or even a bunch of bucks.

Most people never realize that the most valuable resource we have is our *__time__*.

It is the ONE thing we can NEVER get back.

We can always make more money, buy more stuff etc... but we can NEVER recoup our time.

Having given 10 precious years to the prison system, time and freedom were ever so valuable to me. No one had to convince me just valuable my time was.

In prison, it was always the simplest things I missed. Going to the store, eating a sandwich, walking around outside at night, having seconds for dinner, driving a car. It was always the simple and regular things that mean so much when you no longer have them.

It's always the simple things we miss when they're gone.

Take it from someone who knows what it's like to NOT have ANY freedom at all. It is the most valuable thing we can achieve! Don't trade it for anything!

Don't waste your time living in the past. Agonizing over past experiences.

Don't waste your time *giving your time* to someone else.

Take a step right now, **learn from your past experiences, and then leave it behind you** as you move toward your goals.

We never get the time we give away back.

Don't waste a single minute of your time reflecting on the past.

Learn and move forward toward your goals.

Lesson #6: Work Harder <u>and</u> Smarter, Not Just Smarter

You hear people tell you all the time, "work smarter, not harder."

It's apparently "the key" to the elusive "millionaire mindset" that allows people to achieve much more in a fraction of the time.

When you wonder how the most productive entrepreneurs, CEOs, and others get more done in a day than you can accomplish in a week, "work smarter, not harder" is often the answer.

But if you really want to get ahead?

You need to work harder and smarter.

If you look at all of the successful business owners, salespeople, artists, etc... you will notice one common thread throughout all of them.

They all had a HARD WORK ETHIC.

Cultivating a hard work ethic is necessary for anybody looking to reach their goals in life.

And this is one of the things I definitely learned from watching my dad. His work ethic was unmatched and he always strived to do the very best job the first time he did it. He prided himself in a job well done and I'm definitely thankful to have witnessed that first hand.

When I came home from prison, I wasn't afraid of good old fashioned hard work. I was willing to do what it takes. Although I had every single door shut in my face when applying for jobs, one of Robin's friends put me to work in his lawn business.

It didn't take long for me to realize that exploiting my beefcake physique was not something I enjoyed, nor laboring for someone else to profit.

49

While this dude was sipping Mountain Dew Big Gulps from the air conditioned cabin of his truck, he had me slinging 50 pound coquina rocks all over some old lady's mansion estate.

I was thankful for the opportunity to work and make some money, but this was also my first real-life experience of *feeling* what I knew to be true about work, profit and success.

In prison I fed myself entrepreneur lessons, success mindset and personal development philosophies, and I was seeing the stark contrast in a very real and tangible way.

While the sweat poured down my face, and the coquina rocks scraped up my bloody arms, I had a very loud internal conversation...

"Wait a minute! I'm not supposed to be working for the man! I'm supposed to be the man. I'm supposed to be the boss."

"Look at me working by the hour. Homeboy is charging his customers according to the value his service provides them, but I'm clocking hours. I can make money for my ideas and creating value. I can build something once and get paid over and over."

Furthermore...

"I don't need to be out here having a heat stroke, doing crap I hate, when there are so many opportunities on the internet! I can literally do anything!"

But there was one enormous obstacle.

I had no idea how to navigate the "new" internet, what the heck social media was, or anything.

Just to put it all in perspective for you, **there was no such thing as Google when I went to prison**. Yes, you read that right. Just imagine, I never knew what it was like to whip open my computer, type something in, and have a world of info at my fingertips.

Who would imagine that today I would be making millions in eCommerce when the whole internet world was created and passing me by while I was in prison? I didn't even know something as simple as ordering a pizza online!

I had never seen or used a gift card.

There was no such thing as YouTube.

Hybrid cars were just a part of some nerd's imagination.

Bluetooth didn't exist.

Internet on cell phones?! Who knew?

Heck, I thought LOL meant "lots of love" (truth: ask Robin, she died laughing!)

There was no such thing as Facebook, Twitter, Instagram, or Pinterest.

Everyday services like Dropbox and Spotify did not exist, and Netflix was just some weird idea that would never work.

There certainly weren't any online marketing platforms and tools like WordPress, Shopify, Infusionsoft, LeadPages, Click Funnels, Wishlist Member, KISSmetrics, MailChimp, Canva, **nor Facebook Ads.**

While I was in prison, not only did Google come out, but the first iPod was invented, the iPhone was released, cameras became standard on every phone, Skype was invented, HD TV and flat screens became the norm, and so on.

There was a plethora of technology created, introduced and even mastered by the masses, all while I was behind bars. I had no clue about any of it. In fact, here's a picture of me during my first 10 minutes of freedom.

The day I walked out of prison, September 7, 2009, was the first time I ever used a cell phone.

At first it seemed a bit overwhelming, but I dug in and learned step-by-step. In order for me to be able to get to '**working smarter**' I actually had to '**work harder**' first. They go hand in hand.

Let me show you what I mean.

Robin and I geeked out on entrepreneur stuff a lot while I was in prison. We learned about business, marketing, and life together. Everything about entrepreneurship (and especially marketing) intrigued us and energized us.

In 2004 Robin got laid off from her job at a court reporting firm, she decided it was the perfect time to take the plunge into starting a business.

She thought...

"I have a specific skillset"

"I have access to the target market"

"I know the industry and all the players"

"I speak the lingo"

"I know the needs and can competently solve them"

"I know what my relevant differentiation is from the competition"

"Aaaaaaaand, I've got a short window of time to collect unemployment to help me get going"

"LET'S DO THIS!"

She started her business doing legal transcription for local attorneys, private investigators, insurance claims adjusters, and the County Sheriff's Department. The business grew to include Mobile Notary Services, medical transcription and "Secretarial Services" (which was essentially Virtual Assistant services, but a VA wasn't a thing yet). She also provided professional résumé writing services.

She was all over the place, no focus, straight hustle. She was *working hard*. The only *working smart* she knew at the time was to leverage her every asset and skill to pounce on opportunities she saw around her.

By 2006, she was operating a physical brick and mortar local biz full-time and earning over 6 figures.

You can see the picture below when she first opened a physical location, the duct tape is still fresh on the sign installation. Right on the corner of a busy intersection, business was hopping.

Unfortunately, by the time my release-date of 2009 rolled around, the economy was tanking, and her local biz was feeling the pain.

This was in Brevard County, Florida where Kennedy Space Center is. The Space Shuttle Program got shut down, real estate bubble was bursting, people were leaving our county in droves. Her business at that time was **completely dependent on the <u>local</u> economy, and well, that sucked.**

Then there was a knock on the door from Florida Department of Transportation notifying her of eminent domain where the state was taking over her parking lot was to expand the road and she would have to move. This double-sucked.

Business was super slow. Meanwhile, a client of hers was in hot pursuit, begging her to work in his newly opened art gallery in Orlando. It was pretty tempting when she could practically demand any salary she wanted.

Knowing I was only a few months from my release date, we talked about all the pros and cons. Would this be selling out? Would this be quitting our entrepreneurial dreams? We were not ignorant of the very real danger of falling into a comfortable situation and coasting along with a nice cushy job.

We decided it was a good decision as long as we kept focus that it was just a stepping stone. Robin put a sign on her business door "by appointment only" and kept the business afloat while she took a job with her client. We figured that when I got home, I could take over the brick-and-mortar biz and start rebuilding it while Robin had a little "safety net".

In September 2009, I came home and we got married in October.

Even though Robin's boss knew of our situation, and gave us $1000 and a bottle of Dom Perignon as a wedding gift... 3 months later, Robin got fired from the job "because she married an ex-con".

Bye-bye safety net.

Soon after we found out we were pregnant!

A lot happened in between there that led to this realization, but we knew the solution to our current penniless problem...

We wanted real freedom. Freedom to run our biz our way. Freedom to make crazy amounts of money despite the local economy or other people's prejudices.

Our dream of freedom existed in the <u>digital economy</u>... Going online.

So, we decided to start "funding our dream"...

What Better Way To Fund Your Dream Business Than Sell Trash On Craigslist?

You can't just up and start an online business when you're currently dead broke (I recall we had literally $40 in our bank account at the time), and when you're jobless, pregnant, and your new husband just got out of prison.

So we started doing something most people wouldn't dare even dream of...

We started flipping trash for cash profits.

We sold junk on Craigslist, on eBay, we did storage unit auctions, garage sales every weekend, you name it.

We had a goal in sight and we were going to do whatever it took to achieve that goal – even if that meant skulking around dumpsters late at night, digging through the trash to find something someone might pay us for.

You're probably thinking, "No way, they didn't *really* do that..."

But I'm strangely proud yet embarrassed to tell you: **Oh yes. We did.**

And that's exactly how we developed our shameless, prideless '**Work Harder**' mentality that served us well during this season of our life and business.

I'm not saying that I recommend you start digging through the trash if you want to start making money. Although, if this is what you need/want to do to fund your dreams, then by all means do what you gotta do!

What I am saying is that hard work pays off.

Hard work alone will not get you a <u>sustainable</u> and <u>scalable</u> business. Actually, I'll share more of the story and how we literally 'hard worked' ourselves right into a trap in just a minute.

But right now I want to illustrate a point that **hard work isn't the enemy**.

Being someone who has experienced both extreme sides of the "working harder' and 'working smarter' spectrum, **they are both equally valuable**.

Hard work has its necessary place to get you to the place of working smarter.

And if you want to achieve your business goals (or any goal in life), you've got to be 100% committed to put in the work. Otherwise, you're going to crash and burn fast and keep looking for the easy way out until you give up on your dreams.

I can honestly say that it was our hustle mentality to do whatever needed doing to get to our goal of building a sustainable and scalable freedom-based online business that pushed us forward.

We used the money from slinging trash to pay our bills, get our business online, and get ourselves into college to increase our technical skillset.

In June of 2010, we were finally online with our first $99 website. It wasn't much, but we used it to start getting our first online clients on Elance doing random virtual assistant things.

Soon after, **things started getting real...**

As we got more clients, we became "idea suggesting machines" for our clients, **consulting with them on marketing strategies** (even though we had no idea at the time that was what we were actually doing).

Our Clients Were Getting Results!

Mike and I had fallen in love with marketing even more. Learning about it was cool. But DOING IT totally got us hooked. The more ideas we gave clients, the more help they wanted, and the more money we would make.

It was a double-whammy of opportunity. Of course it created more revenue for us, but essentially, we were also given a 'big budget playground' (of other people's money) where we tried, tested, measured and proved as many ideas and strategies as we could think up. We found out firsthand what *actually* worked and what "hot new strategy on the scene" was a flop.

The more experience we got to prove or disprove strategies, the better results our clients were getting because we employed what we knew worked, and rejected the hoopla with strong conviction to save our clients unnecessary heartache.

Our little online VA business turned into done-for-you marketing services where we specialized in marketing support for all kinds of clients – from solopreneurs to mega millionaires.

Naturally, with results like the ones we were getting, clients were lining up. We were '**working harder**' than ever. And it was serving us well.

We had gone from selling trash to earning over 6 figures (again). We even had a waitlist of high value clients begging us to take their money.

And that brings us to the 'working smarter' side of the spectrum...

On Christmas of 2012, we were busy turning our clients into millionaires.

We were doing "done for you" marketing services for our clients. Sales pages, landing pages, funnels, webinars, launches, emails, graphic design, web design, you name it.

I imagine that Christmas our clients were skiing on top of the Alps, or escaping the cold weather and enjoying an island vacation, or some cute freakin' stuff like cuddling up in front of cozy fire with their loved ones without a care in the world.

Meanwhile, on a mountaintop in Michigan, we were literally working our butts off to give our current clients the kind of freedom, fun, and happiness we had been dreaming about from day one of entrepreneurship.

We couldn't take a real vacation because we had too many client needs to manage over the holidays. Instead, it was a "work-cation" to visit family.

Robin's family lives in an insanely small town in Michigan with population of about 500 (I'm talking a little one blinking traffic light, kind of town).

We were out in the middle of nowhere, on the top of a mountain, and surprised to find out upon our arrival that there was that there was no Internet.

We had to take a long haul up and down this big mountain, driving into town every couple hours to hop on the Internet and take care of business.

It was a long drive, and since we're Floridians, we have no clue how to drive in the snow. I kid you not, every single time we ended up getting the vehicle stuck in the snow and had to wait for someone to come tow us out.

Hours a day were wasted. We were emotionally and physically drained, and officially bummed out on what was supposed to be our happy vacation.

That's when it hit us – That's when we had the '**working smarter**' epiphany.

We didn't own our business anymore. Our business owned us.

We were making craptons of money, but we were constantly strapped for time, burnt out, and completely miserable.

Even one tiny thought about our strong family values or all the "plans" we had to homeschool and be an ever-present influence in our kids' lives, made us want to cry. We didn't see how that junk was going to happen NOW.

We reached "money goals" but the reality of our life was not even close to the vision we had when we started down the road of entrepreneurship.

It was painfully real just how **UNscalable** our business was.

We ROCKED at what we did. We had a waiting list of clients who wanted to work with us, but if we took on one more client, we'd literally implode!

Our business owned us, and we were its prisoners.

We knew it was time for a change. We created time-freedom and leverage in three areas; our business model, our acquisition systems, and our sales & marketing systems.

We have since given our '**working smarter**' transformation a name, and the "F3 Framework" is something that we actually teach entrepreneurs around the world in our group coaching program.

We created a *foundation* for freedom by designing solutions to help unlimited amounts of people, where we don't trade dollars for hours.

We created sales and marketing *funnels* which get people to say yes to those solutions faster than I say yes to a frosty craft beer.

And we use Facebook ads to *fuel* and automate the whole process so that there is a steady flow of leads, clients and cash at all times.

Today, we are part of the 'working smarter' crowd.

We have no limit on the amount of people we can help, we enjoy tons of free time, work very minimal hours, are able to give back to the community, go on *real* vacations as often as we want, we can up and go help a friend in need at the drop of a dime, play with our kids all day long, engage in hobbies, and get fulfillment out of life by giving ourselves to any and every cause in the world we are led to, all while millions of dollars of revenue comes pouring in at the same time.

This was our dream.

This is what every entrepreneur dreams of.

But anyone who tells you that you can start 'working smart' and instantly be where we are **without** 'working hard' is a liar and only out to scam you.

The harder you work, the more experience you have, which gives you tremendous insight into how to work smarter.

You need a balance of both.

And you need to enjoy the ride and give it your all no matter which season you're in.

Lesson 7: Breaking the "Roller Coaster" Success Cycle *(You Can Win or You Can Learn, there is No Lose)*

If you're like most people, at least in the 'entrepreneurial' space, you're on a "Success Roller Coaster."

It works like this...

You see a new opportunity, you have a new idea, or you create a new, exciting goal for yourself.

For a few days or weeks, you devote all your energy toward that goal or opportunity. Maybe it's a relationship, a business venture, a new job, a hobby—it can be *anything*. It's a goal you have that leaves you *fulfilled*, happy, satisfied, and *feeling successful*.

But then, the inevitable always happens.

Adversity strikes, the opinion of someone else shuts you down, and "reality" strikes you in the face, leaving you stranded, alone, and falling.

All the excitement when you are "at the top" of the success roller coaster, picturing your future, your fulfillment—all of it fades away and you fall back into the doldrums of day-to-day life.

It's like those pesky New Year's resolutions. You mean well, right? You 'mean' to hit the gym regularly but then life kicks back in.

Look...

You can break out of the roller coaster success cycle that holds so many people back.

All you have to do is follow the 7 lessons I've provided in this book.

Put yourself in control and accept the responsibility you have over your life. Choose your mindset, craft it, and design it around your focus. Chase opportunities and watch them come to you as soon as your mindset shifts. Be thankful for your past, learn from it, and leave it behind. And always work harder and smarter.

Now I know (and you have to accept) that trying to fight through all the B.S. life throws at us is going to hurt.

You can try to dodge it, but you will hit it eventually.

Someone will tell you "you can't."

Things will go wrong.

Lots of things will go wrong.

You'll face adversity and the downward spiral from excited about a new opportunity to depressed and stuck will start threatening to throw you off the "success high" you're on.

But what you need to do, right now is realize: **In life, you can win or you can learn. There is no lose. That very realization is what allowed me to turn a 10-year prison sentence into a catapult for success.**

What it's important for people to realize is that *the pain you go through actually makes you stronger.* The more you're willing to put up with, the stronger you will be and the more you will achieve.

During my stay in prison, I spent a tremendous amount of time working out.

Although that is actually a very common activity in prison (insert TV-induced stereotype), my number one reason for such devotion was far beyond the physical gain.

You see, rigorous and devoted exercise requires a certain mental toughness and I knew deep within me that mental *toughness was tantamount to success.*

While I faced hordes and hordes of haters, naysayers and even saboteurs, the opposition only worked to fuel my drive and devotion.

Every time I would lay down on the bench facing a new weight goal it seemed I would attract masses of negative haters.

Funny thing is, it never once dissuaded, discouraged or derailed me.

It only fueled me.

Being an entrepreneur is very similar to being in prison (except we have better food out here ☺) in that your rigorous devotion and unabashed drive will attract hordes of naysayers and even those who wish to see you fail. Maybe right from within your OWN family.

And just like prison, being an entrepreneur flies in the face of the common and the comfortable norms around all of us. And sometimes it makes those on the outside uncomfortable because it may challenge them as well.

So what!

Do it anyway!

Let the hating, doubting, challenges and failures become the fuel that develops the mental toughness that is REQUIRED.

I was recently contacted by a good buddy of mine who was one of the ex-inmates to whom taught Spanish.

He was one of the few who applied himself and actually learned the language.

Here's what he shared:

"I have been wanting to hang out with y'all for the longest I've just been a little ashamed because I'm not doing as well as what I need to be doing and I look at you all man and that's what I want. I want to be successful I want to help people I want to break the cycle. I just feel like I've been on a treadmill for the last couple of years' u know the old adage two steps forward and 3

steps back such is life but I'm ready to go forward have a good night brother."

The thing that stuck out to me was that in his message he mentioned **"*breaking the cycle*"** (and wanting to help others as well), meaning he had been reading my posts and was <u>inspired </u>to reach out because I was sharing the story.

Your struggle becomes strength. Your strength becomes victory. And the journey becomes a story.

Never underestimate the power of your struggle, strength and story, and its ability to set people free.

"Breaking the cycle" applies to a lot more than just prison.

People all over are trapped and imprisoned by the way they think, by the cubicle, by lies they tell themselves, etc...

If just one person is inspired and set free because you embraced the journey, **it's totally worth it.** I'm sure you may realize that it wasn't easy for me to open up, be vulnerable and share this story. It's real. It's raw and it shines light into dark places. But I knew deep within me that folks needed to hear it. People needed to see what was possible and that circumstances do NOT have the power to dictate your future. YOU DO!

Go out there and break the cycle.

It will be tough.

It will require work.

And you will fail, lose, and learn from your experiences.

But keep your head up and keep moving forward, no matter what.

Remember, in life you can win, or you can learn—you only lose if you stay complacent.

In the almost 7 years since my release from prison I've enjoyed many successes. Successes that I would have never thought possible if I hadn't shifted the way I think. I, together with my lovely wife Robin, have been able to grow several businesses online past the million-dollar mark and have had the great privilege of helping 1000's of other entrepreneurs (just like you) achieve success and freedom in their lives as well.

If you're ready to start learning, winning, and moving forward with your life, I encourage you to join me at www.FromPrisonToProsperity.com/bonus.

Book Mike for Your Media Event

I am a proud father, husband, entrepreneur,
and author. But more importantly, I help people overcome
adversity and learn how to live with purpose, integrity, and clear
goals.

Not that many years ago, I woke up in prison after a long night
that I couldn't even remember. That day, I made a commitment to
seek out and live the
purpose I was put here
for... and to help others do
the same... no matter what
they've done or where
they've been in life.

I love sharing my story
with other people and
connecting with the
community around me.
And I love that my story
has helped countless
entrepreneurs, students,
prisoners, and many others
to experience the same
kind of transformation that
I was fortunate enough to
have in my own life.

If you want to see real,
lasting, positive change in
yourself, your team, or
your organization, you need to contact me now – I only have
limited availability for:

- **LIVE EVENTS**

- **PODCASTS**

- **RADIO SHOWS**

- **BOOK SIGNINGS**

Here's the email address to contact me about a booking:
media@fromprisontoprosperity.com

Mike has been featured in...

BUSINESS Forbes YES MAGAZINE FLORIDA TODAY iHeart RADIO

PRISON GLOSSARY

Let's have some fun...

My story covered a lot of ground inside a Florida State prison. If you haven't caught on yet some of the terminology inside the prison fences is much different than out here in society. So I've put together a 'Glossary of Inmate Terms' for you to enjoy! Here ya' go:

1. Get there/put your boots on – This is the term used to 'call someone out to a fight'. If there is a heated discussion and things get heavy one (or both inmates) will say 'get there' or 'put on your boots' meaning 'let's fight'. This is one of the more serious 'inmate idioms' as it can only be ignored to your detriment. This term is used very seriously and has serious backlashes if ignored.

2. Be 21 about it – this term refers to 'acting like an adult' or owning up if you did something wrong. Instead of allowing the whole dorm full of inmates to suffer punishment for something one inmate did the offender would have to 'be 21' and confess to the officer, or pay the price.

3. Ear hustling – the act of being nosey, snooping or butting into an inmate conversation

4. Turf – referring to free society or life outside the prison walls

5. Hater – someone who is jealous, envious or inwardly desires to see the demise of another but often masks it behind skepticism, criticism or pronounced doubt

6. Old timer – an inmate who has been in prison for more than 10 years or an inmate who has made a career of coming in and out of the system

7. Vizzo – slang term for visitation

8. Jake – inmate code word for officers and guards

9. Recall – this refers to the institution wide activity of reporting back to your dorm or cell in preparation for count time.

10. The yard – the outside recreation area within the prison walls

11. 3rd yard – this term refers to the 'daylight' savings time of year when the sun sets later in the day allowing for the inmates to go back outside in the 'evening' for more activity. It is called 3rd yard because the day is broken down by meals so this is the '3rd' (or after dinner) yard time. Also one of the most coveted times of the year.

12. Chow – adopted from the military this refers to meal time. Also note that 'chow' is required to be consumed within 4 minutes.

13. The corner – the designated area in the dorm or cell block where fights take place. This location is generally selected because of the limited visibility from the guard station

14. Lock & sock – this refers to the weapon created when a master lock in placed inside a sock and then tied off at the end

15. Shakedown – the unexpected rush of officers to perform a massive, dorm wide search. This usually involved the officers spewing everyone's property all over the dorm resulting in hours of search and perusal to find all of one's items again.

16. Jail/the box – slang terms for confinement

17. Sleep late lose weight – a common inmate idiom referring to sleeping in and missing breakfast

18. Parachuting – this referred to an inmate who hopped right out of bed the very moment breakfast 'chow' was called and who completely skipped brushing his teeth

19. Suitcasing – the act of smuggling or hiding items in one's anal cavity

20. Running a ticket – refers to the inmate who runs, manages and distributes the 'inmate' gambling tickets. This usually was a sports related gambling venture.

21. Buck – the slang term for prison made wine. Usually consisted of a potent mixture of rotten fruit, water and sugar.

www.ingramcontent.com/pod-product-compliance
Lightning Source LLC
Chambersburg PA
CBHW071422040426
42445CB00012BA/1263